5 Easy Steps to Build a Brand with Impact

Chris Paradies

ISBN: 1941102239
ISBN-13: 978-1941102237

Published by paradies/inspire®

Volume 1 of the "Lessons from an Intellectual Property Attorney, Entrepreneur and co.Starters Facilitator" series

DEDICATION

To my wife,
who inspires me

CONTENTS

no hype branding

Paradies IP

lessons from an intellectual property attorney, entrepreneur & co.Starters facilitator

INTRODUCTION

Lessons, in life and in business, can be learned the hard way or the easy way. I have been blessed to learn many of the hardest lessons the easy way, by counseling hundreds of entrepreneurs during more than 15 years as an IP attorney. I am offering this powerful FieldGuide, so, you can learn from my experience.

This book is a FieldGuide, because you'll want to carry it with you and refer to your research notes as you continue to grow your brands in the "field." You'll benefit most if you return frequently to add to your branding landscape. This FieldGuide complements my "IP gardening" and "Own what you grow!" programs. You'll benefit more from those programs by completing these 5 easy steps first. However, even if you don't participate in one of my other programs, you'll still benefit from completing the exercises in this book. If you enjoy this book, then you'll enjoy my free, live video training entitled "No Hype Branding," which is a 90-minute webinar that reinforces the five steps and provides additional exercises and greater depth in some of the concepts in this book. Go to http://nohypebranding.com to find out the date of the next free livestream training.

In the next few pages, I will distill for you and your business the lessons that I have learned about building profoundly impactful brands.

FOREWARD

Are you the owner of small business or the prospective owner of a startup? Are you concerned that you haven't done enough to protect your ideas, creative expression and innovation from copying and theft? Are you trying to build a brand that adds sales and increases profit? If you relate to any of these, then, read on. This FieldGuide™ is for you.

Even CEO's of successful corporations will benefit from reading this short, on point guide, but you, as a small business owner, can't afford the time to read most business books that ramble on and on about nothing practical. You've got a business to run. You're the chief cook and bottle washer.

If you are like I was, just a few years ago, then every hour spent working on your business is an hour that you aren't getting paid for working in your business. In a few minutes, this FieldGuide will give you 5 easy steps to take that will build the value of your brand.

I am going to refer to both goods and services as "products" in these pages, because this FieldGuide is equally valid for a company selling goods at retail as it is for a life coach selling services to clients in 45 minute increments.

Let's get right to it.

STEP #1: TALK WITH YOUR CUSTOMERS

Have you ever missed the mark when buying a gift for someone special? Maybe you picked something that you like, rather than something she likes. You men know what I am talking about!

It's the same with customers. Don't assume that you know what your customers want or need.

I am a facilitator with a co.Starters program in Florida. This grass roots program helps people start successful businesses at the local level. Talking with your customers or prospective customers is the strongest tool in the co.Starters curriculum. I have seen what happens when a new or existing business owner starts talking with their ideal customer. The entire business focus changes.

Are you thinking that this is too easy? Actually, this is the hardest step in the 5 step process of this FieldGuide. You'll need to get up courage to go out and listen to your customers. It is not hard if you know how to talk with customers and what to ask them.

First do some homework. Who is your ideal customer? What does your customer do for work and for fun? Where does your customer hang out? How can you approach your customer? Now that you can find your customer. Ask for a meeting or take your customer to lunch.

Start by telling them you are looking to start or grow your business. In 30 seconds, tell them a bit about your background and why (not how) you want to help them. Then, ask your customers (or potential customers) some questions.

What would you change if you could start your company all over again?

What problems do you have that need a solution, right now?

What irritates you most?

What is your top priority this week, this month, this year?

What keeps you up at night?

How much would you pay if you had a solution that could make ________________ go away?

Just like in co.Starters, I'll assume that you are using 3M PostIt® notes for writing down the answers to these questions. The yellow sticky notes show where you should paste your notes. You can have a large number of notes stuck to the pages of this book or only few. It is not the quantity but the quality of the notes that will make a difference in your business.

You might be surprised by what your customer says. Listen for a problem that needs to be solved, immediately. Then, set aside some time **on your own** to brainstorm. Think of creative ways that you can provide your customer a solution to a compelling need or desire.

Is it a need or desire that has been around for a long time without any solution?

While you're listening, you might get an idea for a future product or service! **Try not to listen with a particular solution already in mind.**

The really hard part is to come up with a product that meets an important and urgent need or desire of your customer at a price that your customer is willing to pay.

Hey! If it was that easy, **someone would have already done it**!

Most likely, you will need to think about **how** to deliver a solution in a way that has not been done before. This is good. Being first in a new product category is a great way to establish a new brand.

If someone is already delivering a product for a need or desire of your customer, why isn't your customer using the existing product?

Ask. Maybe you customer didn't know about the existing product. A follow-up call or meeting should be welcome if you have found a possible solution from a third party.

What does your customer like and not like about any existing products? Is there an opening for a new product or way of delivering an existing product? Remember a "product" can be a good or a service. Can you add value to an existing product by delivering it in a different way? That's what Zappos, Amazon and eBay do.

Your product might meet some need or desire that your customer never recognized before you provided your product. This is common for new product categories.

If your customer hesitates to pay for a third party solution that already provides a solution to the problem, why?

Enter the answers to these questions here. This is the beginning of your market research about your competitors' products.

You'll want to know everything about your competitors' products. How much do they charge for their products? How do they advertise? How do they sell? How do they deliver their products to **your** customers? Is there an opening for your product with **your** customers, because your competitors' products don't meet **your** customer's needs or desires?

To your customers, there might be just an "irritation" or some undecipherable longing that you discover during your customer interviews.

You can't stop now.

You have to find a way to reach your customers with your product. You have to find a way to deliver your product to your customer at a price your customer can afford. Go back to your customers if you need more information. By talking with your customers, you will be developing a relationship. Don't overdo it. Be respectful of your customer's time. However, your customers should welcome your interest, if you make clear that you are looking for a solution to his or her problem and are not selling or preselling some product that you have already in inventory.

Continue asking questions until you get the information that you need to **focus** on providing your customer's compelling need or urgent desire. Make solving **your** customer's problem your **focus**. You don't have to reach **ALL** of the potential customers in a particular market. You just have to reach **your** customer -- the one that needs your product and is willing to pay the price that you are asking.

I use the singular word customer, here, on purpose. At this point in your market research, you should be developing a relationship with each customer, one at a time.

Focus on solving his or her problem.

Sometimes, it is a unique combination of features that makes your product distinctive. In your market research, you should identify if your customer wants or needs some unique combination of features, such as ease of use, ability to customize, availability on a particular device or other features.

What **benefit** would having the right combination of features provide to **your** customer? Would it give your customer more time in his or her day? Would it add to the bottom line? Would it give your customer a competitive advantage?

A good way to start is to find out what your customer likes and doesn't like about any existing products?

When you have spoken to enough customers, patterns could emerge that will let you know if there is a market for **your** solution. More importantly, you might be able to identify a particular market segment that will want to buy **your** product, rather than your competitor's products. This market segment becomes **your** customer.

How will your reach **your** customer? Where does **your** customer look for information? Where does **your** customer hang out, when not looking for information? Is there a way to reach **your** customer?

Write down the problem you are going to solve for your customer and how you will solve it.

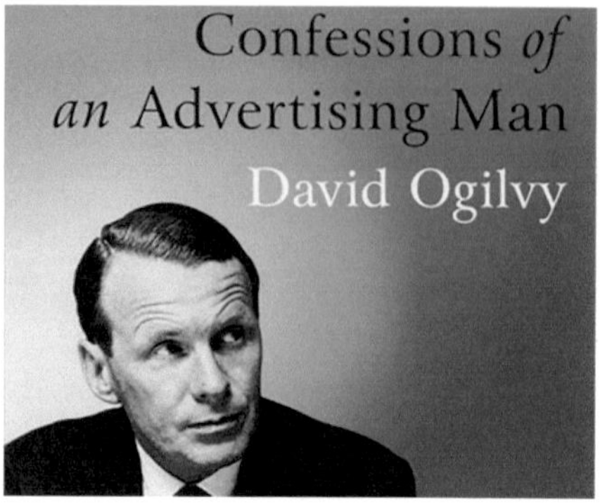

STEP #2: WHAT IS **YOUR** BRAND?

What is a brand?

Did you ever watch the show "Mad Men"? My wife and I watched a bunch of episodes on Netflix -- mostly in a couple of marathon sessions. We enjoyed how it portrayed NYC, our previous home. Mad Men also reminded me of my time as a partner in big law firm, with all of the office politics and personalities. But, the most interesting part of the show was the mix of art, business, psychology and sheer hutzpah of the ad execs and copy writers depicted in the show!

David Ogilvy, author of Confessions of an Advertising Man, is a prototype for the "Mad Men" character Don Draper, the creative ad executive and former copy writer, war veteran… Ogilvy is known as the father of modern advertising. He started out in the business as a copy writer but ultimately changed the way that the ad business looks at customers.

Ogilvy's definition of a brand was the "intangible sum of a product's attributes" in the consumers' minds.

A brand is not your company name. This is a common misconception.

The "intangible sum" is what a consumer remembers about his or her experience with a company and its products, and it becomes a company's or product's brand, for better or worse. In trademark law, this intangible is referred to as "good will."

You have completed STEP #1, you'll know your customer's mind. Now, answer the following questions.

How do you want your customer to feel after purchasing and using your product?

How can you design an experience that delivers that feeling?

Have you looked at all of your product's attributes from the perspective of your customer? (Use as many sticky notes as you need.)

- Company branding:
- Product branding:
- Product packaging:
- Product delivery:
- Product price:
- Product history:
- Product advertising:
- Product promotions:

One way to bring everything together is to focus on your customer in your advertising and promotions.

Another way is to emphasize the core values that you share with your customer in branding, advertising and promotions.

Yet another way is to show your genuine interest and desire to create a positive experience for you customer or to help your customer solve a problem, irritation or serious pain point in your customer's business.

Regardless, it is THE SUM of your customer's perceptions about your product and your customer's relationship with you that will become your brand, for better or worse.

How is your product sold? How is it delivered? How do you provide customer support? How do you introduce new products to existing customers? If your entire company, marketing strategy, product development and customer support does not personify its brand, then you will not OWN your brand.

How will you bring everything together to deliver your product in a way that resonates with your customer?

STEP #3: A COMPANY OR PRODUCT BRAND?

I've been asked: "What is most important, a company's brand or the brand of its products?" There is not one, simple answer to this question. Brand powerhouses, such as Apple and Procter & Gamble (P&G), apparently take opposite views on this topic, at least on the surface.

Apple's management is organized as a very large tech startup, designing software and hardware in and for computers, smartphones and wearable devices. Apple has made its mark with its strong company branding that has some referring to it as a cult. Its iPhone brand is much less important than its Apple brand.

P&G is hardly known by consumers, but I'll bet you know at least one of its 50 or more iconic brands: Tide, Bounty, Ivory, Downy, Gain, Luvs, Max Factor, Mr. Clean, Nice 'n Easy, Puffs, Secret, Swiffer, Tampax.

P&G's branded products are sold at retail to its customers, primarily women, at grocery stores and pharmacies. P&G uses traditional advertising on TV and other media that is designed to make an emotional connection with its customer. Coupons and other promotional incentives entice consumers to give the brands a try, and the consistent quality of P&G's brands and targeted advertising take over from there.

Its product brands are more important than its company brand.

Apple's Story

Apple has chosen to reach its customers with its company brand. Look at its product "brand" names: iPhone 6, iTunes, iPad, Apple Watch, Apple TV, Really? You couldn't get more descriptive (except for the Apple moniker) and get a federal trademark application approved! It is the company brand that sells Apple's products.

Apple has been a successful company. Few would care to argue this point. Yet, Apple's iPhones capture less than 20% of the global market share for smartphones. But, market share isn't everything. Apple takes home more than 90% of the profits generated by all smartphone sales, worldwide. The other 80% of smartphone sales share less than 10% of the remaining profits in this product category.

How is this possible?

Before Steve Jobs returned to Apple, the company had lost its focus. It was selling too many products and had lost any meaningful differentiation from its competition.

According to Jobs, Microsoft had won the PC wars, and Apple was months from going broke. His return resulted in changes at Apple. He became the lead evangelist for the Apple culture. Apple, the brand, was going to mean something again.

The question at the time was whether Apple could even survive. Jobs hadn't been that successful since leaving Apple. Could he turn the company around? Apple discontinued many of its product lines and focused on making the remaining products better, more distinctive, more Apple.

Apple focused on the future, on elegantly designed products for its customers, those creative people who "think different". By the way, Jobs has his name on more than 300 patents. Apple is an innovative, forward-looking, technology company.

Jobs required the company to think about the customer experience and work back from there to design the hardware and software. A revolution in technology was coming. Jobs anticipated this and bet on iTunes, iPod, Mac Air and eventually, the iPhone and iPad, creating a platform for this new technology, the "app".

As a result of this focus on its customer, Apple went from nearly broke to a market cap exceeding that of Microsoft. Under his leadership, Apple made many controversial decisions. Jobs said that these decisions were easy, because his focus was on providing elegantly designed products for Apple's customers.

Microsoft might have won the PC battle, but Apple is in the process of winning the war, taking computing to hand held and wearable devices and transforming software from Microsoft's model of all-in-one, integrated business productivity suite to individual "apps" for solving specific problems, mostly developed by third party developers.

Apple makes every effort to design consistently elegant customer experiences for all of its products. Apple's brand stands for extraordinary attention to product design for people who care.

P&G's Story

P&G sponsored the first "soap" operas on radio in the early twentieth century in order to sell its brands of soap products to American housewives. As America moved to television, P&G produced and sponsored TV "soaps". P&G's programming resonated with American housewives, establishing an enduring emotional relationship, while advertising its high quality branded products.

I grew up in the 1960's and 1970's, and I knew not to disturb my mom when she was watching As the World Turns. This was mom's time, and my siblings and I knew better than to interfere. My first name, Christopher, actually comes from a character's name in mom's soap opera, which was sponsored by P&G. So, now you know why P&G really made it into this FieldGuide. It has had a direct impact on my life!

Even today, P&G is in the forefront of producing and sponsoring media that has the ability to reach its customers, emotionally. P&G has always been careful about the programming it chooses and is looking for new ways to reach its customers as media and entertainment are changing.

As the World Turns was considered to be "conservative". P&G discouraged the more scandalous story lines found in some of the other soaps. Nevertheless, it was #1 in day time TV for 20 years, from 1958 to 1978. You have to stand for something, and when you do, then you reach your customers.

My mom went to be with the Lord in 2004. Her soap continued on the air only another six years after her passing, until 2010. In 2014, the Cincinnati News reported that, as a result of the great recession of 2007-2008 and its lingering effects on consumer spending, P&G would sell or abandon about 100 of its 180 brands.

The remaining 80 brands generate 95 percent of P&G's profits. According to P&G, after trimming the non-performing brands down to the 80 leading brands, P&G will be much easier to manage and operate.

P&G is a company that focuses on its product brands. Its customers trust its branded products. If P&G has an under-performing brand, it improves, sells or discontinues it.

Market share and margin are important to P&G's management, and P&G tracks these metrics. P&G makes every effort to produce the leading brand of products in each of its product categories, giving consumers what they want in those product categories and developing new product categories that did not exist, previously. P&G is its brands.

Comparing Apple and P&G

How could two companies have such different brand strategies and both be successful for so long? Both struggle against stiff competition from "generics".

For P&G, the number of product categories and changing consumer preferences make it impossible to have a single company brand. Instead, P&G focuses on developing iconic branded products for each of its product categories, and develops a relationship with its customer via its programming, which resonates, emotionally with its customers, providing a perfect platform for advertising its branded products.

For Apple, its company brand is built on its consistent attention to detail in the design of a distinctive consumer experience for all of the products it sells. The products can change over time, even the product categories will change, as technology changes, but Apple, the brand, remains.

P&G has focused its branding on developing a relationship

between its brands and its customers through radio, television and, now, digital media. Apple has focused on developing a relationship between its brand and its customers by designing a unique customer experience.

Both P&G and Apple have found a way to connect with their particular customers. Both have developed brands that resonate, emotionally with their particular customers. Both make great products that satisfy their particular customers' needs. For P&G it is all about trust. For Apple it is about the Apple experience.

You have a very short window to capture your customer's attention.

Given all of this, what one thing do you want your customer to remember about your brand? Write it below.

Decide now to set your mind on developing a coherent brand strategy, and read on!

STEP #4: CHOOSE A BRAND THAT RESONATES

True or false: Customers commit to buy a product or service on emotion, first, and justify their decision, later, with rational thought.

TRUE!

Your customer will remember his or her emotional connection with your brand long after the rational reasons for their choice have left the station.

Why resonate? What is resonance?

An acoustic guitar is an example of resonance. The vibration of the strings are amplified and prolonged by vibrations of the guitar's sound box. When you hear your favorite guitar solo, you feel the chords, emotionally. The music resonates not just in your ears but in your mind, your heart, your very being, long after the performance is complete.

Your emotions amplify and prolong the experience. This is "emotional resonance." That is what you want for **your** brand.

Broadway musicals and blockbuster movies know how to use music that resonates, emotionally with you. These commercial products use music thematically during their productions in order to set an emotional tone and to have an enduring emotional connection with the audience.

Brands have an emotional response, too.

If you are going to develop a profoundly impactful brand, then you will need to establish a brand relationship that emotionally resonates with your customers.

How could someone get emotional about your product or service? Write down emotions your customers feel about your brand.

So, how do you pick a brand name that has emotional resonance™?

I recommend "Hello My Name Is Awesome" by Alexandra Watkins to my clients having trouble selecting a brand name. Go to http://ipgardening.com/amazon to buy the eBook. It is a 98-page fast read that will give you a quick crash course in choosing a brand name.

A brand name with legs permeates a company's branding strategy.

It inspires your slogan, company job titles and the jargon that you use to describe your products and that your customers use in interacting with your company. Go to http://IPgardening.com to see an example of branding with legs.

So, what makes for a brand name with legs? Consider the following guidelines.

- It must be different than any competitors' brand names.
- Short, memorable names beat long descriptive ones.
- The spelling should be easy or easily remembered.
- Get a .com domain echoing the brand name.
- It must not cause confusion with any other brand.
- It should be used consistently and continuously.

It is now common to have fun with your brand. For example, you can select employee titles, such as Communications Ambassador or Innovator in Chief, and other themes that reinforce your brand. Your brand is a story told through the totality of your customer experience.

Consistency is easier if your brand is closely tied to your company's core values, the personality of your brand.

Preferably, any brand names that you choose should be suggestive of your company's personality or an important attribute of your company's product or products.

However, a brand name should never be merely descriptive of a product.

A brand name must be distinctive, i.e. unlike any of your competitor's brand names. There are many examples of distinctive brand names that have developed strong emotional responses, for better or worse: Dolby, Xerox, Exxon, Nike, Ikea, Pixar, google..., the list is endless. On the top of these distinctive brand names, companies have attempted to build a relationship with THEIR customer, to resonate emotionally. Some have succeeded. Others failed.

Your colors, music, images, layout, logos and slogans that you choose should be distinctive, also, and round out your brand story.

What is a brand story? It is a satisfying explanation of what your brand means and how it came to mean what it means. It helps your brand to have an impact that resonates, emotionally.

Impactful brands require attention to detail in shaping consistent, continuous experiences that resonate emotionally with your customers. Impactful brands permeate your company.

Let me give you some examples.

McDonald's

McDonald's restaurants are the same nearly everywhere, are inexpensive, satisfy kids with "Happy Meals" and give moms a break from the kitchen. "You deserve a break today at McDonalds." McDonalds' customers are moms and dads that have had a busy, productive day. Its food services provide mom and dad with an out, because you deserve to skip cooking a meal at home. It's not gourmet. It's fast. It's easy.

McDonalds chose a clown character, Ronald McDonald, as the owner of the McDonalds surname, rather than a real person. Ronald and a cast of characters figure into a plot line akin to a Punch and Judy show. Ham"burgler" is dressed as a thief/convict, and Ronald and his friends prevent the nefarious intentions of Hamburgler.

This theme is woven into the décor and packaging, making McDonalds a fun place for kids. It is a safe place for kids to eat a Happy Meal™ with a toy inside and other menu items appealing to young kids.

This theme attracts kids. Parents follow with their purses.

McDonalds gets an A for consistency. You know what to expect when you go there. The only surprise is what toy your child will receive in his or her Happy Meal™.

Zappos

Zappos provides exceptional selection, unparalleled customer service and a return policy that can't be beat.

Empowered employees are "Delivering Happiness™" in every box. Zappos is "Powered by Service™" and works hard to convince its customers to be passionate about its brand. In order to prove authenticity, the owner published a book of unedited essays submitted by its employees about the culture at Zappos. Some companies try to build a myth, but a myth only works if it is based on some truth. Zappos' customer service representatives are instructed to go above and beyond to provide a "wow" factor.

Zappos' brand name was derived from the Spanish for shoes, zapatos. Apparently, this wasn't good enough. The owner of Zappos has been quoted as suggesting: "A lot of people actually think our name comes from the fact that we ship so fast – like we zap your order to you."

A brand name doesn't have to be suggestive of any attributes, but customers like to have some justification for the choice of a brand name (even if the marketing story comes later). Zappos has an "all of the above" brand strategy. It does it all.

Starbucks

Starbucks has come up with its own language. It has added words to the lexicon. You order a "tall" instead of a small from a "barista" who can create a "skinny caramel macchiato." Is there coffee in that???

Starbucks has their own music mix tapes, which are played (and sold) in trendy bar lounges with Wi-Fi access. The colors are green and coffee tones. Yet, the décor is fresh. It's cool. It's hip. Well, you get the idea. Starbucks thought about its customer experience, and it did something right.

According to the company, the brand name is inspired by Moby Dick (the book, presumably, not the whale). The name "evoked the romance of the high seas and the seafaring tradition of the early coffee traders," according to the copy on their website. (Starbuck was the first mate on the Pequod in the book Moby Dick, for those of you, like me, who read the book long ago.) Starbucks, the brand, weaves this story into its story of the founding of the company.

Starbucks focuses on its **customer experience**.

Spanx

SPANX®
BY SARA BLAKELY

Spanx story is about a "local Tampa girl done good," who created a new category for women's undergarments. Sara Blakely invented the category of comfortable shaping undergarment. More importantly, she came up with a great brand name, Spanx™, for her new product. Sara made it really big when she appeared as a guest on Oprah, when Oprah was big. It was a product brand for a one product company, but now, Spanx™ is becoming a company brand.

A myth has been created about the brand and its originator, Sara Blakely that appeals to professional women. The brand name, itself, is a little naughty and is somehow suggestive of posteriors. Any number of Hollywood and reality TV starlets have had their Spanx™ exposed at one time or another, apparently, which has not hurt sales of these undergarments at all.

Spanx uses a playful brand name and targets a solution to a pain point of its customers, a less than flawless body. Its patent is of secondary importance but suggests an innovative solution unlike any previous attempts, such as girdles.

Sara opted for free advertising by being the face of the brand. This paid off when she was invited as a guest on the Oprah show.

Spanx focused on a **solution** to its customers' **pain point**, a perceived less than perfect shape, defining a new category of more comfortable, sculpting undergarments for women.

All of these brands, McDonalds, Zappos, Starbucks and Spanx, are successful. Each has defined a new product category. The first three delivered existing products in a new way, defining a new category of service. Spanx defined a new product category and delivered it through traditional retail channels.

All of them have, or have created, a story to explain the brand name and to tie together the brand name with the other elements of their brand. All resonate with customers, emotionally. All appeal to their particular customers, authentically. All have chosen colors and slogans that go with the brand name. All have developed a brand personality that fits the brand name.

Most have developed their own jargon, whether a meal is a "Happy Meal" or delivering a shoe order is "Delivering Happiness" depends on more than a company brand name. The entire relationship between the customer and the brand's product needs to deliver on its promises to its customers.

Write down several brand names, based on the brainstorming exercise described in "Hello My Name Is Awesome" by Alexandra Watkins.

STEP #5: BE ATHENTIC; BE A LEADER

Your brand or brands can't be all things to all people. Does anyone remember "New Coke"? Coca Cola tried to out sweeten Pepsi, back in the 80's? Reacting to slipping market share, Coca Cola launched a big ad campaign about a change to its traditional Coca Cola formula. Naturally, Coke drinkers hated it! It was such a flop that people wondered if the entire affair was some sort of marketing ploy to sell more Coca Cola "Classic". Coca Cola denies this. It is a cautionary tale. You can't change "The Real Thing" that your faithful customers like, in order to capture your competitor's customers.

Genuine

-- A brand is a promise, and you will have to deliver on the promise, consistently, in order to have a brand that resonates. --

Your brand will only resonate positively with your customers, if the brand is authentic, originating from your company's DNA. Anything phony won't work. Impactful brands are **genuine**.

Apple's iPhone is successful by reaching 20% of the market. P&G is happy only when its brands are #1 or #2 in each product category. Both companies make quality products that meet their particular customer's needs and desires. A softer tissue and a faster screen update are not so different when viewed in light of providing the customer what the customer wants, even if the customer doesn't know that he or she wants it, before it is provided.

Both Apple and P&G are genuine. Apple is genuinely focused on its customer experience. P&G is focused on being first or second in safety and quality in each brand category.

Focus

Whenever a brand tries to be all things to all people, it tends to lose focus, sales and profits. Tom Hall is the Hall in Tucker Hall, a well-respected PR firm in Tampa. In his book, Ruthless Focus, Tom gives examples of companies that lose their focus and flounder. It is very common for a company to drift away from its core mission, as it grows.

When Steve Jobs returned to refocus Apple on its core values, Apple's brand became distinctive, again, and Apple succeeded beyond all expectations by ruthlessly focusing on customer experience. P&G refocused on its brands by jettisoning a hundred underperforming brands and concentrating on its 80 remaining brands.

If these companies, which make great products, can lose their focus, then you could lose your focus too! Focusing on what sets your business apart from its competitors is critical. How will you do that? A strong, distinctive brand can keep you focused!

Distinctive

Ask yourself. How am I different than my competitors? Use a SWOT analysis (which is broken down below) to help you determine internal strengths and weakness and external opportunities and threats. Then, use this analysis to determine how you are distinctive. Can your brand name and other brand elements highlight your distinctive strengths or the distinctive benefits that your customer receives from his or her relationship with your brand?

Strengths

Your strengths are what you do well, already. These are not aspirational traits. Instead, critically self-assess and determine what areas you, or your company, are best in class.

Strengths can be technical, educational, experiential, financial, organizational, operational, social.... You get the idea. Strengths can be sustainable or fleeting. If you have a technical solution that is better than anything out there today, it can be outdated tomorrow by changes in the market, technology, competition....

Maybe you don't see yourself or your company as best in class in any particular area. Do you have a combination of better than average characteristics that might be considered a strength? Strengths are not measured in a vacuum. Your average rating might be significantly better than your competitors' poor ratings. This could be considered a strength.

Being critical doesn't mean that you have to be negative about your abilities, but you do need to be realistic. Sometimes, it is a good idea to ask others what they think your strengths are.

List your strengths here:

Weaknesses

Weaknesses are your internal flaws or things that your products currently lack, compared to your competition. Your weaknesses could be in your processes, talent, distribution, marketing, funding… Again, this is self-assessment time, but if you need help, ask your wife, friends or mentors. Just don't hate them for being honest.

Why is this important?

Your customers will identify your weaknesses. You want to have an answer when they do. Can you shore up your weaknesses? Is it impossible to make your weaknesses strengths? No. It's not impossible, but it can require hard work.

If someone asks: "Is it true that you only have 5 employees?" What if you answer: "Yes, and that is why we work 10 times harder and listen 10 times better than any of our competitors with hundreds of employees. We value your business." Well, this only works if you really do work 10 times harder, listen 10 times better and really do value their business. List your weaknesses, here:

Opportunities

Opportunities can be anything originating outside of your company that has the potential to benefit your company. These can change over time. Both positive and negative external events may offer opportunities. Some examples are:

- Changes in technology, e.g. Apple and the iPhone.
- Changes in the marketplace, e.g. Amazon online sales.
- Changes in government policies, e.g. Obamacare.
- Events, both local and global, e.g. BP oil spill.
- Economic booms or busts, e.g. the great recession.
- Demographic changes, e.g. aging baby boomers.
- Failures of your competitors.

List your opportunities here:

Threats

Threats can be anything originating outside of your organization that has the potential to harm your company or its brand. The opposite of any examples listed as possible opportunities could be threats. It just depends on whether it helps (opportunity) or hurts (threat) your company.

List your threats here:

You don't have to be the size of Apple or P&G to brand like Apple or P&G. Are any of your distinctive attributes something that will resonate with your customers, emotionally?

I am sure that you all know that you'll never be able to reach ALL customers with a single brand. If so, that is a good thing. Instead, your one goal is to reach **your** customers. If you find **your** customers, they will want to do business with you over and over again.

Genuine, Focused, Distinctive

Remember the guidelines for a brand with legs?

- It must be different than any competitors' brand names.
- Short, memorable names beat long descriptive ones.
- The spelling should be easy or easily remembered.
- Get a .com domain echoing the brand name.
- It must not cause confusion with any other brand.
- It should be used consistently and continuously.

How will the totality of your customer's experience with your brand or brands encourage an emotional resonance that is genuine, focused and distinctive? Now is the time to put it all together. Based on your customer interviews, how will you grow a branding landscape that consistently reinforces your brand story? Remember the brand attributes.

- Company branding:
- Product branding:
- Product packaging:
- Product delivery:
- Product price:
- Product history:
- Product advertising:
- Product promotions:

Will your brand focus be on your company brand or on your product brand? Some companies, such as Spanx, start with a product brand and try to transition the product brand to a company brand.

Apple grew its company brand and diminished the importance of its product brands, over time. Its Macintosh brand (a famous type of apple) was not followed by other apple varieties. Instead, it was shortened to Mac, and it now only survives, barely, as part of Apple's

MacBook Air brand of laptop computers. Some of Apple's product brands are pretty descriptive and rely on the Apple logo for distinctiveness, such as Apple TV. See below, for example.

Others, such as P&G, grow the value of their product brands. Focusing on developing a relationship with their customers through emotional resonance of programming. The programming is selected to appeal to their customers. Emotional resonance between P&G's product brands and their customer develops through the medium that P&G chooses to advertise its brands. Then, P&G builds trust by consistently providing brands that provide the highest levels of safety and quality compared with other brands and generics in the same product category.

Let me provide an example.

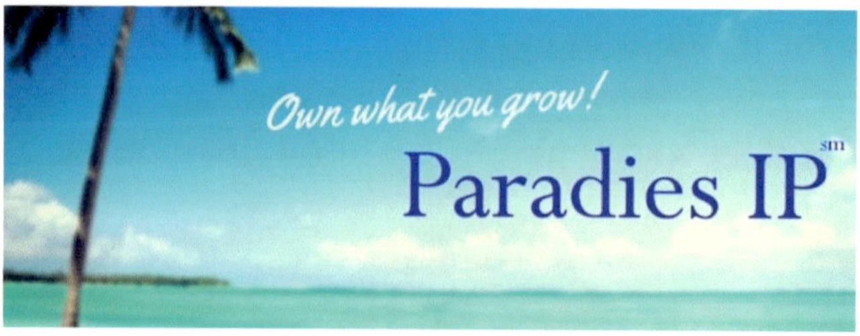

Paradies IP™

Paradies IP is based on my core values: to love my God with all my heart, mind and strength and to love my neighbor. My family name, Paradies (pronounced paradise) means *"a place of complete contentment, peace and joy."* Peace, contentment and joy are not what most small business owners experience on a daily basis, but Paradies IP will help you to move forward in that direction.

In the Bible, a thief being crucified on the cross next to Jesus, asks Jesus to remember him, when Jesus comes into His kingdom. Jesus, beaten and dying on the cross to save all of us, says "Truly I tell you, today you will be with me in paradise." Even while suffering terribly, Jesus knows where he and this thief are heading. Nobody is beyond God's redemptive grace and love. It is freely given to all who believe and call on the Son of God; He who gave his life for us and rose from the dead three days later. That is why I am a Christian.

That is why I love my neighbor, because **He** first loved me.

I've always been involved with creative ideas, new technologies and leading edge concepts, even when I was an artillery officer in the U.S. Army, back in the 80's. I fielded the TACFIRE fire direction system in my first battalion. Then, I was among the first to field light TACFIRE, the sequel, as the battalion fire direction officer in my second unit.

After I left the army, I went back to school and earned a Ph.D. from Rensselaer, worked as a scientist and engineer in Europe and as senior technical specialist and program manager at a large aerospace corporation. I went to law school at nights for about a year, before starting work as a legal intern and patent agent for a large intellectual property law firm in New York City.

Working within large institutions, large companies and big law firms laid a foundation, a foundation of intra-preneurship, which I define as working within an organization to offer new products.

However, I prefer life as an entrepreneur, because I have a chance to make a real difference in **your** life. If you let me, I can help to set you free. Free to follow your passion. Free to work, not just **in** your business, but **on** your business. To grow it. To own it.

I practice what I preach.

By following my own advice, I can continue to volunteer and lead various organizations and programs helping startups and early stage companies, as a co.Starters™ facilitator, as a mentor in Mentor's Corner™, at Startup Exchange™, as Chair of the Board of Directors of the Tampa Bay Innovation Center (TEC Garage℠) and as the chair of the EDI2 program for Hillsborough County. There is a theme here that has developed over more than 15 years helping business owners both in my work and as a volunteer. Helping you **is** my passion. This is how I love my neighbor.

I say this as an example of how to align your passion and your products, not to boast. My treasure is in heaven, and I am not looking for accolades here on Earth. Instead, I look for ways to serve. By helping **you** to find success in your business, I am serving my God. I am helping to change lives. Your life. Your employees' lives. My employees' lives.

I have learned a great deal participating in the successes and failures of literally hundreds of small businesses and a few very large companies. I have learned much from founding and operating several of my own businesses, a law firm, a publishing company and Paradies IP. This depth and variety of experience is my strength. I have aligned this strength with my heart in my vision to help you and others like you to grow the value of **your** brands and **your** IP.

I can't offer complete contentment, peace and joy. The "shalom" or "all is well" of Paradise is granted by God, alone, through His Son.

That is the good news. But the programs of Paradies IP can, at least, give you some peace of mind that you have done what needs to be done to create, protect and grow **your** brand and **your** IP.

This is the best way for a startup to succeed, ultimately. Failing to secure your startup's IP risks losing everything. All of your hard work can be copied or stolen by others. By creating an **impactful** brand and using your company's IP to **own, protect and grow** the value of your brand, you'll be ready for success.

Look at my websites: http://IPgardening.com and http://ownwhatyougrow.com. The Paradies® brand, the image of a palm on a beach, with a blue sky, IPgardening, FieldAlerts, PestAlerts, the images, the colors, Own what you grow!, ... all of it, combines to tell a story. All of this fits with my mission statement:

"To offer the small business owner the peace of mind that comes from knowing that he or she has done what is necessary and prudent to own, protect and grow the value of his or her company's intellectual property and to transfer that value to a distinctive, impactful brand."

I want to help you own, protect and grow your intellectual property and your brand.

-- *If you don't own your IP, then somebody else does!* --

It is my mission to help you avoid the mistakes that others have made. By building the value of your IP, you build value in your brand! An impactful, distinctive brand add sales and increases profits in your business. This is the bottom line. Your brand is the sum of your customer's experiences with your company and its products. An impactful, distinctive brand drives sales of your products. Your marketing and sales departments are there to reinforce your brand and to remind your customers of the need to take action. This is the essence of "*No Hype Branding. No Hype. Just Help.*"

How are you going to build your brand story?

Build Your Brand

So, now you have a brand that is distinctive. What do you do next?

You make it your own.

You live it. You protect it and guard it from imitators. Yes, you are going to need a trademark or trademarks to protect your brand. You are going to need a domain name, preferably related to your registered trademark. You are going to need to copyright your website, promotional materials, software.... You will need to protect your know-how and innovations. You will need imagery, colors, slogans, jingles, graphic design... all the elements that go into building your brand value.

All of this is protectable intellectual property. All of it is owned by somebody. I say again (and often):

-- *If you don't own your IP, then somebody else does!* --

You'll put systems in place to guarantee that your startup owns all of its intellectual property, and you'll transfer the value of that intellectual property to your brand. My Own what you grow! program can help. You don't want a buyer's due diligence team to be the first to discover that your company doesn't own its most valuable assets, its IP. Even if you can correct it at that point, you will have left a ton of money on the negotiating table – not to mention the attorneys' fees you'll pay to fix the problem.

You'll let your customers know about your intellectual property, and you'll guard against any misuse of your brand and your intellectual property within your company and by others.

You'll promote your brand, developing a relationship with your customer. Your customer, each individual one, will come to trust your brand, because you consistently deliver products and services based on the values of your company that you share with **your** customer.

Your customer will know that your products and services benefit them in ways that your competitor's products and services do not, and they will be willing to pay what you ask. You'll add sales and increase profits by solving **your** customer's urgent needs and desires, reliably and faithfully, every time.

Imagine developing a team, each member of your team being passionate about his or her part in your business.

You'll truly own the company that you're growing. It might not be "Paradise," but if done right, you will feel at peace, knowing that you have done what **you** could do to own, protect and grow the value of **your** brands. Of course, you'll need to watch for new opportunities, to improve your solutions and to solve new problems for your customer, always with your brand in mind.

Let's start!

By now, you might be feeling overwhelmed. Don't worry. Most entrepreneurs feel this way, at least some of the time. If you don't have the resources to hire someone, then just take one step at a time, when you can make the time. I can help, but you need to make the time to consult with me one-on-one at my law firm, Paradies Law P.A. or by becoming a member in the programs offered by Paradies IP. (Paradies IP is not a law firm.)

3 things you can do now!

1. Fill out the sticky notes in this FieldGuide.
2. Register for my free, online branding training.
3. Like Paradies IP on Facebook and get inspired.

Own what you grow![sm]

If you can't afford the tens of thousands of dollars needed for an IP attorney to create and implement an IP landscape for your business, then start with the *Own what you grow!* program at http://ownwhatyougrow.com. This video-on-demand training is my IP master class. You'll learn how to own, protect and grow your IP and to transfer the value of your IP to your brand. Each video lesson is accessible and has a call to action at the end that will help you take one step at a time to create your IP landscape plan and to put your plan into action. Enrollment for the Own what you grow! program is only available during open enrollment periods.

IP Gardening[sm]

When you have developed your branding plan, then you'll want to sign up for my IP gardening program. You will need FieldAlerts™ and PestAlerts™ for your trademarks and domain names. These alerts help you to remember important dates, such as renewals, and warn you about dangers that could damage the value of your intellectual property (IP) rights. You will receive FieldAlerts™ via email, exactly when you need to tend to your IP. These FieldAlerts™ will include a short video that explains what you need to do and how to get it done. These concise videos, which we call "Shoots™" are directly on point, because they are meant for you. This helps you to decide on the best course of action for **your** IP.

"Timely information that helps me take immediate action to protect and grow the value of my IP, brilliant!"

Just go to http://IPgardening.com to sign up for an affordable Field pass. We offer a bundle for IP gardening and Own what you grow! at a significant discount. Just sign up for one or the other, and we'll send you the bundle offer, when it's available.

ABOUT THE AUTHOR

Chris Paradies is an intellectual property attorney, registered patent attorney, entrepreneur, co.Starters facilitator, author and international speaker. He created the *Own what you grow!* and IP gardening programs for business owners in response to a demand for timely, concise information needed for his clients to take action to own, protect and grow the value of their intellectual property (IP). Chris graduated from West Point, earned a Ph.D. from Rensselaer Polytechnic Institute, and received his law degree, *summa cum laude*. He has advised hundreds of businesses about IP and branding for more than 15 years. He is a frequent speaker on topics relating to IP, and he provides live, online video training about branding and IP, including a live, 90-minute training entitled *No Hype Branding*. He is passionate about helping business owners, especially small business owners, and volunteers as a mentor at TEC Garage, as a co.Starters facilitator and as the chair of the board of directors for the Tampa Bay Innovation Center.

Made in the USA
Monee, IL
05 November 2026

67379443R00033